BOOST

SUPERCHARGE YOUR CONFIDENCE

JASMIN KIRKBRIDE

Vie Books is an imprint of Summersdale Publishers Ltd

Summersdale Publishers Ltd
46 West Street
Chichester
West Sussex
PO19 1RP
UK

www.summersdale.com

Printed and bound in Croatia

ISBN: 978-1-84953-977-7

Substantial discounts on bulk quantities of Summersdale books are available to corporations, professional associations and other organisations. For details contact general enquiries: telephone: +44 (0) 1243 771107, fax: +44 (0) 1243 786300 or email: enquiries@summersdale.com.

CONTENTS

INTRODUCTION

Most of us would like to be more confident in one area of our lives or another. You might be a brilliant linguist, but struggle as soon as you have to speak in front of a large audience. Perhaps you love your work, but wish you were bold enough to push for a promotion. Maybe you could simply do with a little boost across the board. Whatever your dreams and desires, with a little effort and a truckload of positivity, you can turn your worries into long-lasting confidence.

Starting the journey towards greater confidence takes courage, and it doesn't happen overnight, but by following the tips in this book you can begin today. Confidence isn't about being perfect, or knowing everything: it's about accepting yourself, adopting a positive outlook and opening the doors to new possibilities. By taking simple steps and learning new skills, you can become a happier, kinder, more resilient and more assured version of yourself.

WHAT IS CONFIDENCE?

Confidence is a state of mind that comes from believing in yourself and your abilities. As with most things, though, the deeper you dig into it, the subtler the definition becomes, so this chapter is a quick guide to the ins and outs of confidence.

WHAT CONFIDENCE IS...

Confidence is your belief in your ability to do something in a particular situation. Having confidence is about learning to trust your skills so that you can do a good job and face new challenges without anxiety. It is also about being able to say 'no' and standing up for what you need.

People will find that they are confident in different areas of their lives, and it's rare for anyone to be confident in their abilities across the board. For example, you could be a very confident tennis player but a less confident cook. While you can raise the level of your confidence in these individual skills, it is also possible to bring up your overall base level of confidence, by developing your belief that even when you struggle to do something or don't even know how, you can learn the necessary skills and get better.

People do not just have 'low' or 'high' confidence: they fall somewhere on a spectrum. There's nothing wrong with your current position on that spectrum, wherever you happen to be. Most of us need a little boost to be more confident every so often, and that's completely normal.

We gain strength,
and confidence, and
courage by each experience
in which we stop to
look fear in the face.

Eleanor
Roosevelt

This journey
isn't about anyone
else: this journey
is about me.

WHAT CONFIDENCE IS NOT...

There are a lot of myths about confidence that aren't always helpful. Having confidence isn't about being perfect and getting it right all the time. In fact, one of the keys to becoming more confident is realising that failure doesn't really exist, because mistakes are always an opportunity for learning and growth. The only failure is to never try at all.

Being more confident is not about fulfilling other people's expectations of who you are and what you should be doing, either. Part of being confident is recognising your own needs and talents and standing up for them.

Finally, confidence is also not an absence of fear. Certain situations still make confident people nervous too – the difference is that they don't let it stop them doing what they want to do.

The quickest way to
acquire self-confidence
is to do exactly what
you are afraid to do.

Anonymous

CONFIDENCE AND SELF-ESTEEM

When we talk about confidence, it's important not to get it mixed up with self-esteem, and to know the difference between the two.

Not everyone agrees on where the separation between self-esteem and self-confidence lies. But in general, self-esteem is how you *feel* about yourself and confidence is about whether or not you think you can *do* something. Self-esteem usually affects every aspect of someone's life, whereas confidence issues can crop up only in certain situations.

It is possible to have high self-esteem but low confidence in certain areas and vice versa. Self-confidence and self-esteem do impact on each other and everybody has their own personal journey in this regard. But if you want to improve your self-confidence or self-esteem, the first step is learning to accept yourself.

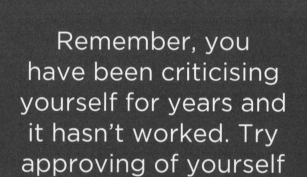

Remember, you have been criticising yourself for years and it hasn't worked. Try approving of yourself and see what happens.

Louise
L. Hay

CONFIDENCE AND ARROGANCE

People often get confused between confidence and arrogance, but they are not the same thing at all. Confidence is knowing your abilities and trusting in them, but arrogance is having an exaggerated view of your skills and importance, or seeing yourself as superior.

Arrogant people are hard to deal with, because they seem to know everything, but what's interesting is that arrogance is often a result of a *lack* of confidence. It springs from an attempt to cover up a person's insecurities, rather than from an excessive amount of confidence.

Most people are a little bit arrogant from time to time. If you catch yourself having an arrogant moment, take a step back mentally, breathe and look at the situation. What are you trying to defend against? Does the other side have a valid point? Can you replace brash arrogance with quiet confidence?

Be humble in
your confidence,
yet courageous
in your character.

Melanie
Koulouris

DON'T FAKE IT TO MAKE IT

Lots of people will tell you to 'fake it till you make it' where confidence is concerned, but this isn't always the healthy option. A little faking here and there can help you get ahead, which is why there is a chapter on appearing confident later in this book. However, true confidence comes from within.

Faking confidence is often a sign of shaky self-belief. People who do this still feel the pull to prove or defend themselves that less confident people often exhibit. Paired with a confident veneer, this can lead them to be quite combative or arrogant.

Truly confident people, on the other hand, have a strong psychological basis for their self-belief. It's quite hard for anyone else to knock them off their perch and, what's more, their confidence grows all the time. It's like a muscle: the more they use their skills, take on fresh challenges and learn new things, the more confident they become. This tends to make them better collaborators and mentors. So don't just fake it: dig deep, embrace the journey, and let your confidence shine from within!

Even when life
gets me down, I
have the strength
to be unshakeable.

HOW LOW CONFIDENCE CAN AFFECT YOU

Low confidence can affect you in a number of different ways. It can hold you back from reaching your full potential, and stop you from trying new things, learning new skills, or meeting new people.

Feeling less confident can make even small, simple tasks feel stressful, causing unnecessary anxiety. If someone feels unconfident about taking an exam, for example, they are likely to worry about it for weeks beforehand, whereas a more confident person might only experience nerves on the day, or perhaps not at all.

Low confidence often comes from a place of thinking badly about yourself. Constantly having to defend against your own inner monologue can be exhausting but – like every other negative effect of lower confidence – you can learn to turn the boat around.

Always remember
you are braver than you
believe, stronger than
you seem, and smarter
than you think.

A. A. Milne

ASKING FOR HELP

Learning to become more confident can be scary sometimes, because you have to take risks and try new things, but it can also be incredibly fun and fulfilling. Even so, if your journey ever feels overwhelming, it's fine to ask for help along the way – in fact, it's the right thing to do. You could reach out to a trusted friend or family member, or go to a doctor or counsellor if you need professional advice. Choose the route that's right for you at that particular moment.

Reaching out for help is not my weakness: it's my strength.

HOW CONFIDENT AM I?

Some people know straight away the areas where they are confident and the ones where they aren't, but for others it can be a little trickier to figure out. That's okay – learning about yourself is part of becoming more confident, but it's always good to know where you're starting from. In the pages that follow there are some tips to help you figure out your levels of confidence.

Everything
you want is on the
other side of fear.

Jack
Canfield

Discover your triggers

Areas where you feel less confident can often create bad moods, anxiety or stress. Start keeping a diary, noting what you've done each day and how it made you feel. Notice the patterns that build up: which tasks make you feel nervous or insecure? These are good indicators of trigger areas where you might have low confidence.

WHAT'S HIGH AND WHAT'S LOW?

To find out your areas of high and low confidence, take half an hour to make a list of memories. Create two columns. Fill the first one with achievements you're proud of and situations where you have felt capable. In the other column, list things you've done that have made you nervous or that you feel you could have done better. If particular skills keep cropping up in one column, it probably reflects your confidence level in that area.

As soon as you trust yourself, you will know how to live.

Johann Wolfgang von Goethe

Your personal confidence journey

Everybody has their own confidence journey. Your confidence in different areas can go up and down throughout your life and, like every area of self-improvement, it's an ongoing process of learning, patience and self-love. There isn't some mystical destination of becoming 'A Confident Person', but if you keep going, your confidence muscles will get stronger and you will become a more confident, happier person.

I will love the
person who is
always with me
on this journey:
myself.

CONFIDENT MIND

Most people think that confidence is all about how you look and behave, but true confidence actually comes from within – from how you think and feel about yourself. Here are some tips and tricks to help you ensure your inner monologue is positive and encouraging.

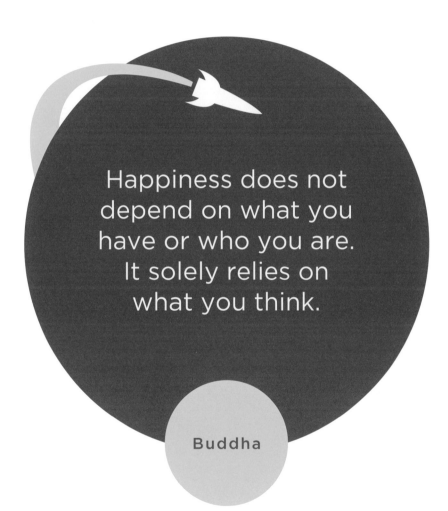

Happiness does not depend on what you have or who you are. It solely relies on what you think.

Buddha

WHAT DO YOU THINK ABOUT YOURSELF?

Everybody has an inner monologue, a series of thoughts they regularly engage with that reinforce how they see themselves. For lots of people, and especially people who suffer from low levels of confidence, these can be quite negative, like 'I'm not good enough,' 'I don't deserve this,' or 'They won't like me.' Often these thoughts aren't objectively true, or they simply exaggerate a situation. The more we hear these negative thoughts, the more we believe them. The more we believe them, the more we say them to ourselves – it's a vicious cycle!

Part of becoming more confident is about taking control of these negative thought cycles and turning them around. The first step is to find out what your negative thoughts are about yourself. Keeping a diary can be very helpful here, or just taking half an hour to write down your doubts and insecurities. Beyond helping you identify your thought cycles, the act of putting them down on paper can be quite cathartic in itself.

If I work hard
and stay positive,
I can do anything
I put my mind to.

Challenging negative thoughts

Once you've discovered your negative thoughts, you can start to counteract them. Write positive, non-pressurised responses to your negative thoughts and say them to yourself when you catch yourself in a negative thought cycle. For instance, if you catch yourself thinking, 'I can't do this,' consciously respond by telling yourself, 'This is challenging, but I can learn to do this.'

Happiness is not a goal.
It's a by-product of
a life well lived.

Eleanor
Roosevelt

If I wouldn't say these things to someone else, why should I say them to myself?

Is it objective?

When you discover a
negative thought, challenge
it head on by asking, 'Why do I
think this? Would I say this about
someone else in my situation?'
Once you start looking at it, as is
often the case with our worst thoughts,
you will probably find that the statement
isn't objectively true. The knowledge that
negative thoughts aren't real doesn't necessarily
make them go away, but it does help us to not
take them so seriously when they do arise.

Building positive thoughts

As well as challenging your negative thoughts, you can also practise positive thoughts. Start by keeping a special positivity diary where you note three things you are grateful for each day, and one thing you think you did well. Reflect and read back over them once or twice a week. You'll soon begin to realise that life is much more positive than you thought – and that your contribution to it is huge!

SLOW DOWN THE TRAFFIC

Human beings have been blessed with this amazing capacity to *think*. But sometimes our brains get into the habit of thinking a bit too much, which can be stressful. Minds that like to keep busy are prone to engaging in negative thought cycles just to fill the quiet spots, but actually quiet moments are okay. Mindfulness and meditation exercises are an excellent way to slow down the traffic inside your head. Not only will your brain grow out of the negative-thought-cycle habit, you'll also make room for more positive thoughts to bloom.

There are a lot of apps and guides for mindfulness out there, but here's an exercise to get you started. First, sit or lie comfortably in a quiet place. Breathe slowly and deeply, consciously relaxing your body every time you exhale, working in little sections from your toes to the crown of your head. Once you feel fully relaxed, begin to count your breaths. Once you reach ten, begin again, really paying attention to how it feels to breathe. If you find your mind drifting, accept your thoughts and bring yourself back to your breath. Simple, yet effective!

Meditation practice isn't about trying to throw ourselves away and become something better. It's about befriending who we are already.

Pema
Chödrön

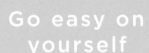

Go easy on yourself

Sometimes we all have negative
thoughts or get busy-brained
– and there's no shame in that.
When you catch yourself thinking
negatively, don't beat yourself up about
it. Don't cling to the thought, or worry
over it – let it pass like a cloud. Accept that
in the moment you felt insecure and move on
without judgement. Nurturing positivity shouldn't
become another mental whip to beat yourself
with: it should be a joyful, loving process.

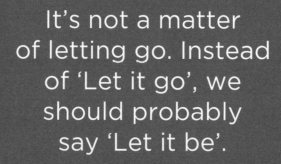

It's not a matter
of letting go. Instead
of 'Let it go', we
should probably
say 'Let it be'.

Jon
Kabat-Zinn

By changing
my thoughts,
I change
my world.

ENVISAGE A MORE CONFIDENT YOU

Imagination is a powerful tool when it comes to positive thinking. Take a few minutes every day to visualise yourself as a happier, more confident version of yourself. Relax, and take several deep breaths. Picture yourself feeling positive and proud of who you are, surrounded by people who love you just for being you. Try not to attach this image to any particular idea of success, like a promotion at work. In this visualisation, you are enough, whatever your achievements.

Nothing can dim
the light that shines
from within.

Maya
Angelou

Know your strengths

People in need of a confidence boost often find it tricky to be objective about what they have achieved, but being proud of something you did well isn't egotistical – it's a very important part of developing self-love. Own the moments when you've done a good job and you can start to enjoy your strengths and the confidence they bring.

There is no chance,
no destiny, no fate, that
can circumvent or hinder
or control the firm resolve
of a determined soul.

Ella
Wheeler
Wilcox

Accept and cherish compliments

Some of us can find it hard to accept compliments. We'll often find ways to negate the remark. For example, if we were told, 'That top looks really nice on you,' we might reply, 'Thanks, but it's really old.' When somebody compliments you, accept it with a simple 'Thank you' and a smile. You can cherish compliments by writing them down, too. Keep them in a jar and pick one out to boost you on a bad day.

I have as much right as anybody else to be loved and appreciated.

Make a proud list

It's important to appreciate what
you've already achieved. Keep a
list of moments that made you feel
particularly proud – you can add past
achievements to this list as well. Read
them back to yourself whenever you need
to remind yourself how awesome you are.
Congratulate yourself when you do a good job and
remember: it's not egotism – you've earned it!

Accept yourself,
love yourself and
celebrate yourself.

Osho

SURROUND YOURSELF
WITH POSITIVE PEOPLE

Negative or positive, your inner monologue is
significantly influenced by what's going on around
you – especially what other people tell you. Surround
yourself with friends and family who believe in
you and make you feel good about yourself, and
your inner confidence will get a huge boost.

Don't let the noise of others' opinions drown out your inner voice.

Steve Jobs

DON'T LET ANYBODY TREAT YOU BADLY

As well as surrounding yourself with positive people, have the courage to step away from those who treat you badly. Whether it's bullies at work or a tricky relationship at home – or even a friend who's just too sarcastic towards you – you have every right not to be belittled, insulted or otherwise hurt.

It can be tricky to extricate yourself from difficult people, but there is always a way. Discuss the situation with a neutral third party, whether a friend, a family member or even a counsellor. Figure out an action plan to talk to the person who is causing you problems, and explain that you need their behaviour to change. In serious cases, you might want to remove them from your life completely. That's a legitimate course of action: if someone is causing you harm, it is not your job to fix them. Instead, look after yourself, have the courage to stick to your guns, and create room for the love and respect you deserve.

I am a beautiful
person from the
inside out, and I
deserve to shine.

Don't 'catch' insecurity

No matter how awesome and positive the people around you are, just like you they will inevitably experience their own insecurities and rough patches. While it's important to support and help your friends and loved ones, always remember which problems are theirs and which are yours. Anxiety and insecurities are easily caught, so be careful not to pick them up from other people.

BE BEAUTIFULLY IMPERFECT

Most of us know that perfect people don't exist,
yet some of us often still expect ourselves to be
perfect. It's an impossible goal that sets you up to
feel like you're failing even if you achieve
amazing things. Instead, do your best in
each given moment and recognise
that that's enough.

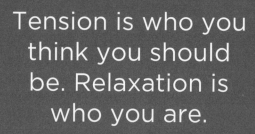

Tension is who you think you should be. Relaxation is who you are.

Chinese proverb

CONFIDENT IN THE MOMENT

Sometimes, even when we're very confident, the moment can just get on top of us. Deadlines loom, the stage lights go on – things can get stressful. But a wobbly moment doesn't have to shake your confidence to the core. Here are some words of wisdom for when the going gets tough...

It is confidence in our bodies, minds and spirits that allows us to keep looking for new adventures.

Oprah Winfrey

PRACTISE MINDFULNESS

One of the best things you can do to help deal with stressful situations is to be mentally prepared for them. Having a daily mindfulness exercise is a great way to help keep your confidence unshakeable even in tricky situations. Just ten minutes of mindfulness meditation a day can help rewire your brain to make it more positive.

Start by finding a quiet room; sit down and close your eyes. Breathe deeply and slowly into your belly. Feel the air as it moves through your nose or mouth, down your throat and into your lungs, then follow its journey back out again. Allow thoughts to crop up when they want to but, instead of getting involved in them, visualise them becoming part of your breath. As you exhale, let the thoughts go with the air in your lungs, and imagine yourself in a state of relaxation and calm.

I breathe in
bravery and
I breathe out
negativity.

Be mindful in the moment

When your insecurities kick off, breathe in and out with awareness, letting your mind drop into that same, soft space you reach when you practise your mindfulness exercises. Remind yourself you are safe – then with each breath, imagine yourself having overcome your insecurity and succeeded in the moment. Whether it's putting pen to paper for an exam, or getting going on a challenging task at work, you'll soon find yourself feeling good about bouncing into action.

STAY POSITIVE

Now is the time to action all that positive thinking you've been working on. Repeat your affirmations, remind yourself of past successes, and give a big smile. Tell yourself that you are strong and courageous enough to overcome your insecurities, that it doesn't matter if you get something wrong, and that every moment is an opportunity for growth and learning. Beat back the fear – you've got this!

I am what I think.

Take a break

It isn't possible in every situation,
but sometimes when we find
ourselves up a creek without a
paddle, the best thing you can do is
take a short break. Set yourself a time
limit to come back and face your problem,
then leave the situation and take a walk
around the block. Get outside and oxygenate
your brain, practising mindful breathing with
every step. You'll feel much more like getting back
to business when you return to your challenge.

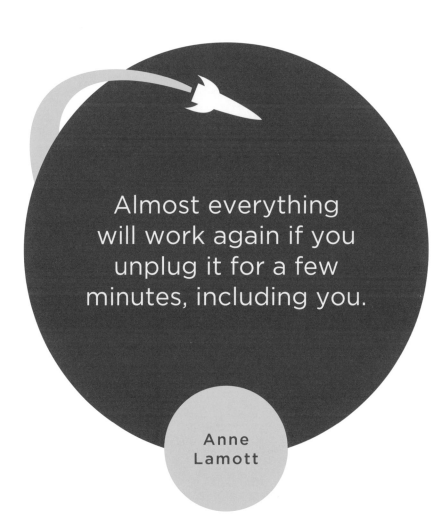

Almost everything will work again if you unplug it for a few minutes, including you.

Anne Lamott

FOCUS ON SOLUTIONS, NOT PROBLEMS

Rather than engaging in cycles of negative thoughts, keep bringing your mind back to the issue at hand. Concentrate on coming up with solutions, rather than dwelling on the problems. And if any problem seems too large, divide it up into smaller, more manageable challenges that can be handled one at a time. If your mind drifts to insecurities, don't berate yourself – just gently bring yourself back to the task without judgement.

Start by doing what's necessary, then what's possible, and suddenly you are doing the impossible.

Anonymous

COMMIT TO THE ACTION

Procrastination is the bugbear of more and less confident people alike, but the truth is that putting off an activity that makes you feel nervous is a sure-fire way to make yourself feel worse. Often when we get around to the tasks we've been putting off, they aren't half as scary or difficult as we feared.

Putting a stop to procrastination doesn't have to be daunting. Be in the moment and commit to action. You don't have to be fast; you just have to do things one little bit at a time. Congratulate yourself often, internally telling yourself you're doing really well – even for the small stuff – to give yourself a positivity boost. Before you know it, the thing that made you feel insecure will be over, and you'll have done a great job getting through.

One step
at a time,
I will achieve
my goals.

WRITE IT OUT

At some point in our lives, most of us will experience a sustained period of worry or insecurity. It could be brought on by a problem at work, in our personal lives, or something else entirely. Whatever the cause, writing out all your negative feelings when you feel them bubbling up can be a simple, cathartic way of releasing them. You can keep the writing private: nobody else has to see it – it's just a way to deal with that negativity.

CONFIDENT BODY

Being confident isn't just about the mind – it's about the body too. And it's not about *looking* a particular way but about how you *feel*. Looking after yourself and making yourself a priority will help boost your confidence across the board.

Take care of your body.
It's the only place
you have to live.

Jim Rohn

Take 'me time'

Taking time out to relax helps boost confidence and positivity. Stress contributes strongly to feeling nervous and insecure, so take a break at least once a day for 'me time'. Have a bath or read a book: this is your time to do whatever you need to do. You don't have to live up to anyone else's expectations – just make sure it's stress-free. Get regular breaks when you're working too. A calm, well-rested mind is much more confident and productive than a frazzled one.

Time for myself is not an indulgence: it's a necessity.

Exercise

Exercise is a great de-stresser, and as you see the hard work pay off as you become fitter, you'll start to feel heaps more confident too. Try to make sure you get in a half-hour work out three or four times a week for optimum results. It doesn't matter what kind of exercise you do, and it doesn't have to cost the earth. If you can't join a gym, try running in your local park, or following exercise routines in YouTube videos. Clubs for team sports and dance are particularly good for growing your confidence around other people, while mindful activities like Pilates and yoga are good for a clean, clear mind. Try to get outdoors as much as possible when you exercise: green spaces are proven to help boost a positive mindset.

YOU ARE WHAT YOU EAT

Eating healthily isn't about going on a diet or cutting out the foods you love; it's about eating the right balance of food so that your body can thrive. When you don't give your body the nutrition it needs, it feels under pressure and run down, worsening physical and mental stress. Although it's tempting to binge and comfort eat when we feel insecure, consuming lots of saturated fat and sugary foods will give you energy crashes and make you feel lethargic.

Turn away from the junk food and pick up some fruit and veg – you should aim to eat at least your five-a-day. Mix them with slow-burning carbohydrates like wholegrain rice or pasta and proteins like nuts, meat, dairy, eggs and particularly fish, which is full of feel-good, look-good nutrients. Make sure the right vitamins and minerals are included in your diet too – and if in doubt, top yourself up with supplements, particularly mood-boosting vitamins A, B, C, D and E. By eating well, you can make your body stronger and healthier, improving your mood and invigorating your confidence.

If you have good thoughts, they will shine out of your face like sunbeams, and you will always look lovely.

Roald
Dahl

You are what you... drink?

Although caffeine may make you feel more productive in the short term, once it's worn off it can cause drowsiness and grumpiness. Too much caffeine can even make you feel anxious. Similarly, the high sugar content in fruit juice and many fizzy drinks can send your mood plummeting. So, if you're looking for a confidence boost, the best thing you can drink is actually pure water. It helps your body run smoothly and keeps your brain hydrated for thinking positively and staying focused.

DRINK LESS ALCOHOL

The big one to watch when we're talking about confidence and nutrition is booze. Lots of people grab a drink at a party to relax them when talking to people, but the truth is that alcohol is not their friend. While alcohol can lower inhibitions, it's actually a depressant, so in the long run it isn't doing you any good. Relying on booze as an essential prop to help us relax into social situations is a risky technique that can lead in the long run to addiction – it's much better to learn to handle the situation without needing what's in the glass. Try replacing an alcoholic drink with a glass of water or juice: you'll still have a comforting object to hold, and something to drink whilst talking, but you won't suffer the negative effects of alcohol.

I am fantastic
just as I am.

GET ENOUGH SLEEP

When you don't get enough sleep, it's hard to concentrate and maintain a positive attitude. What's more, sleep deprivation can make you feel pretty wired: it's your body's way of telling you to lie down and take a break. If you have trouble sleeping, try staying away from screens for at least an hour before bed, get into a regular bedtime routine, and practise mindfulness exercises focusing on breathing and relaxation as you're falling asleep.

FEEL GOOD ABOUT
HOW YOU LOOK

Adopt a positive attitude towards your body. Tell your body you love it – even the bits you might be insecure about – and appreciate what it can do. Your body works so hard! Body confidence isn't always easy, but self-love is a good place to start.

Wear clothes that make you feel confident and happy, and take care of your appearance. You don't have to break the bank on a thousand-pound watch or wardrobe revamp: it can be as simple as ironing your shirts or brushing your hair – taking care of how you look will help you feel confident as you go out into the world.

LIVE SIMPLY AND CLEANLY

Living simply is a clever trick to boost body confidence: working and operating in clear, clean spaces helps your body feel like it's got room to breathe. Have a sort out and send your old junk to the second-hand shop. Keep your home and workspace clean, tidy and organised. Studies show that people who live simply find life easier – and when tasks are easy to do, your mind and body feel naturally more confident.

CONFIDENT
APPEARANCE

Even when you're not feeling your most confident, you can make other people believe that you are, and in some situations, like meetings or interviews, that can be all that matters.

Show up in every single moment like you're meant to be there.

Marie Forleo

Dress the part

A great way to instantly boost
your confidence is to dress the part.
Wearing a smart suit to a job interview
or a gorgeous outfit to a party tells other
people that you think you're worth a million
bucks. You don't have to spend loads on
new clothes – just wear something that's clean,
neat, appropriate and makes you feel fantastic!

I am confident,
I am brave, and
I am worth it.

USE CONFIDENT BODY LANGUAGE

Experts estimate that a whopping 55 per cent of all our communication is done through body language. People are having whole conversations with you before you even open your mouth. That might sound intimidating, but it's actually something you can take control of relatively easily and use to your advantage.

To give an impression of confidence, stand tall, with your shoulders back and your head high, but not so high you're looking down your nose at people. Keep your body open by avoiding crossing your arms in front of you. Breathe slowly and deeply, and consciously relax. Don't fiddle with your hair or face or bite your nails or lips, as these will highlight your insecurities. When you talk with someone, make regular eye contact, though be careful not to stare as this might intimidate the other person. Nod gently and listen carefully; this will offer positive reinforcement to the person you're conversing with, and subconsciously it will boost you too.

At first it may feel strange to change your body language in this way, but it can make a huge difference to how others see you – and to how you feel about yourself.

Beauty begins
the moment you
decide to be yourself.

Coco
Chanel

Speak up

When we're nervous we
automatically talk faster and
at a higher pitch than normal.
Concentrate on slowing down your
words, annunciate clearly and relax
the vocal muscles in your throat to lower
your voice. Don't be afraid of silences
– they're a natural part of conversation –
but make sure your voice gets heard: your
ideas are just as valid as everyone else's.

I have a right to be heard and my opinions are valid.

SMILE!

You don't have to give a huge cheesy grin
if you're not feeling it, but a small smile lets
people know you're listening and engaged,
and that you're feeling happy and confident.
This is a trick that creates real well-being too:
smiling releases all sorts of lovely endorphins
that make you feel happier, more relaxed
and more confident. Best of all, smiling
is contagious, so you'll start contributing
to everyone else's good mood.

FIND AN ANCHOR

An anchor is something that gives us a feeling of stability in uncertain situations. A good-luck charm is an example of an anchor, but they can also be gestures, phrases or habits – some of which we may not even be consciously aware of.

Some of these unconscious anchors can lead to people looking insecure: biting lips or nails, clicking pen lids on and off repetitively, picking at skin, etc. Instead of engaging in these actions, consciously find an anchor that helps you feel safe, while occupying that busy, insecure part of your mind.

The best anchors are ones you can action by yourself, without having to rely on any external objects. This way, your anchor will always be available to you whenever you need it. Try doing a small gesture when you feel really good, like holding your thumb in a lightly clasped fist. Your brain will begin to associate it with good times. Then, when you do the gesture during a tense moment, you'll subconsciously remember all the times you felt great and your confidence will soar.

Just believe in yourself.
Even if you don't,
pretend that you do and,
at some point, you will.

Venus
Williams

Be comfortable in your skin

Some people change their appearance in public: they might dye their hair, put on make-up and perfume, or wear figure-shaping underwear. If you find these things help you to present a confident front, go for it, but don't feel pressured into doing them. Being confident is not about conforming. It's about knowing your needs, standing up for them, and feeling comfortable and proud in the skin you're in. This goes for everyone – men and women – aged fifteen to fifty and beyond.

True confidence
comes from within.

CONFIDENT LEARNING

Confidence isn't about being perfect all the time. In fact, more confident people are often good at being open about the things they struggle with. Confidence isn't just about knowing you can do something – it's also about realising you can learn to do new things and get better at them.

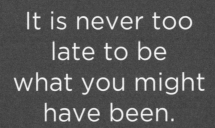

It is never too
late to be
what you might
have been.

George
Eliot

ALLOW LIFE TO HAPPEN

Most of us have dreams we'd like to achieve and places we'd like to get to, and achieving goals is a really important part of becoming more confident. However, it's also important to hold these dreams lightly: if they don't happen, you haven't failed. Life just happened in a different direction.

Everybody has multiple futures inside them. Just because you have a vision of what one of those futures might look like, it doesn't mean it's the best one, or that you should shut yourself off from other ideas. When you're learning and growing through life, you're constantly opening up doors to new people and new possibilities. Embrace them. It's okay to change your mind about what you want.

Low confidence can lead to beliefs like 'I'm not in the place I am supposed to be', but thoughts like this can stop us fulfilling our potential. Instead, wherever you are right now, appreciate the moment and the road that brought you here.

Dreams are important, but so is the here and now.

Tear up your inner rulebook

Confident people don't necessarily experience less anxiety or fear about new things or difficult situations – they're just better at overcoming them. They're used to pushing their boundaries just a little bit, taking in new ideas and experiences and learning from them. Tear up your inner rulebook about what you're capable of and embrace the learning experience. Get uncomfortable. Fear isn't always bad – sometimes it's just a natural part of inner growth.

I can learn
to grow despite
my fears.

LEARN TO LOVE LEARNING

Culturally, we're often brought up not to like school, but it's time to turn that idea on its head. Embrace the learning process, even when it's really challenging you, and take pride in your work. Tell yourself how much you're looking forward to your class or training session. Invest in new stationery to make the learning experience feel more special. Realise the teacher is there to help you, read around your subject, and slowly but surely you'll feel your attitude begin to change.

Learning new skills and being open to change can bring fantastic things into your life – often things you never knew existed. You might fall in love with a new industry and take a new career path, develop a passion for pottery or poetry, or decide it's time to move towns. Whatever new dimensions learning brings to your life, embrace them.

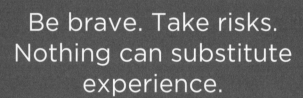

Be brave. Take risks.
Nothing can substitute
experience.

Paulo
Coelho

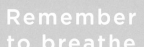

Remember to breathe

Learning and growing is a big ask and as exciting as it is, it can also feel tough at times. If you catch yourself feeling wobbly, unwind into the moment. Breathe deeply and consciously relax as you would in a mindfulness meditation. Tell yourself that you are perfectly capable of doing what needs to be done and remind yourself of past achievements. Take a few minutes out if you need to: it's okay to ask for time and space.

Not knowing is
not a failure:
it's an opportunity
to grow and learn.

DON'T FAKE KNOWLEDGE

The number one tip if you're learning something new is this: don't fake knowledge. Other people who are more knowledgeable in the area you're discussing will always find out – eventually. Humility is a great quality in confident people. They can accept that they don't know everything, and there's absolutely no shame in that. Rather than trying to pretend you know about subjects you're unfamiliar with, ask questions about them.

Invest in your wobble-spots

Take the areas you're less confident about and invest in them. Commit your time and energy to teaching yourself new skills and improving on existing ones. Practise the things that make you nervous. Join a club or attend classes if you can. If you're unconfident about public speaking, practise in the mirror at home or sign up to a local debate team. Push your boundaries gently but persistently. Improvement and confidence will come.

If you want to conquer
fear, don't sit at home
and think about it.
Go out and get busy.

Dale
Carnegie

SET GOALS...
AND SMASH THEM

Set yourself goals for the things you would like to achieve. Start small and work your way towards something bigger. Do you want to be a better dancer? Begin by setting achievable goals – to practise once a week for ten minutes, for instance. Build it up until you practise every day, before increasing the amount of time you practise for. Make a goal to join a club that will help you. By taking small, consistent steps, the final result will be huge.

You can use similar techniques to overcome stressful tasks. Stress can make you feel overwhelmed, so break down large projects into small, achievable chunks. Not only will you feel like you're doing a lot, you'll also get through lots of them in a smaller space of time, so it will feel like you're achieving loads. Congratulate yourself on every single step towards your goals.

I've got this.

FEEL FINE ABOUT LOOKING SILLY

Don't worry about getting things wrong or looking silly – making mistakes is a normal part of the learning process. It wouldn't be a skill if everyone could do it straight away. Stay calm and accept constructive criticism gracefully. Know that the person giving you feedback isn't trying to make you feel bad – they're trying to help you to get better.

Always be a first-rate version of yourself, instead of a second-rate version of someone else.

Judy Garland

Stop comparing

It's very tempting to compare ourselves to others, especially when it comes to learning. We can get really competitive about exam grades or physical achievements like getting a new belt in a martial art. This often leaves us feeling glum and inadequate.

But you can stop the shame spiral. When you feel that you're getting sucked into the comparison game, remind yourself of a recent happy memory or an event you're looking forward to, and remind yourself that *your* life is awesome too. Appreciate that, whatever our skill levels, we are all equally valuable in our own unique ways.

Everybody brings something unique and wonderful into the world – including me.

LISTEN

Quite often when we're learning, we fail
to listen properly. We tense up because the
new information we're being given is a big
unknown and can challenge what we know,
which can be a little scary. Next time you feel
that way, know that your ego doesn't need
to get riled. Breathe in deep and relax
your posture. Allow new information
and insights to enter your mind.

Confidence comes not
from always being right
but from not fearing
to be wrong.

Peter T.
McIntyre

FIND YOUR POWER PLACE

As unsure as you might be in some areas, the
likelihood is there is at least one thing you know
you're good at. That skill will probably have
a particular place you associate with it: if it's
cooking, it might be your kitchen; if you're a
good reader, it might be the local library. Find
the place that makes you feel like you're in your
element and visit it when you feel in need of a
boost. The good vibes you associate
with it will help you feel ready
to tackle anything.

Prepare

A lot of the time we know a
situation is coming up where
we might not feel completely
confident. There is one big thing you
can do to help feel more secure about
it: prepare. Do your research beforehand.
Write down the key times and places you
need to know. And – as always in a situation
that makes you nervous – practise, practise,
practise! Knowing you've prepared before your
big day – whether it's an exam or an interview – will
give you not only a boost, but an edge as well.

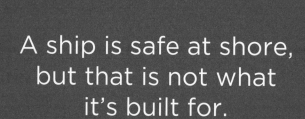

A ship is safe at shore,
but that is not what
it's built for.

Anonymous

BE A 'POSSIBLEIST'

Optimists think everything is going to be wonderful, pessimists assume the worst will happen, realists try to get an objective view on things – and 'possibleists' think anything is *possible*. Unlike optimists, they don't *expect* everything to turn out wonderfully, but they know that it *can* be great if they work hard and maintain a positive attitude. Adopting a possibleist outlook will help your confidence: you know you can get there – all you have to do is keep going.

I believe
everything is
possible – all I have
to do is start
the journey.

Practise affirmations

As you're learning, it's important to remember your goals and keep up your positive thinking. One way of helping to keep worries at bay is by practising affirmations. Instead of letting the 'I can't' or 'It's too hard' thought cycles prevail, repeat to yourself 'I can', 'I will', and 'Through hard work, this is possible'. In time, you'll believe it to your very core.

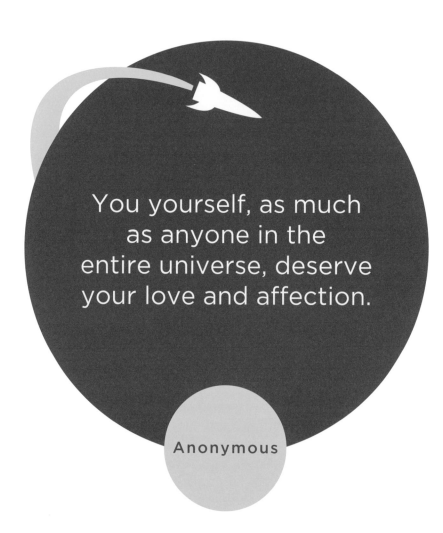

You yourself, as much as anyone in the entire universe, deserve your love and affection.

Anonymous

CONFIDENT IN THE WORLD

Confidence isn't just about improving your skills and believing in your own worth, it's also about being able to go out into the world, set boundaries and stand up for what you need. Here are some top tips to help you stand up for yourself.

The more you praise
and celebrate your life,
the more there is
to celebrate.

Oprah
Winfrey

DISCOVER YOUR WANTS AND NEEDS

Knowing what you want and need can be a hard thing to figure out, especially for less confident people, who tend to worry about getting in other people's way. Yet, a lot of the time when we feel insecure, it's precisely because we're not getting our needs met. Take time out to figure out what you would require to feel more confident in a situation that makes you uneasy. Do you need more time to do a certain task? Do you need more training to meet the requirements of a new responsibility at work?

Whenever you need to feel better about a situation, write it down and figure out what actions you can take to meet those needs. Be imaginative with your solutions – and then be brave in asking for them to come to fruition. Chances are, your requests are reasonable, and your managers, mentors or peers all want to support you to do your best and be as happy as possible.

It is legitimate
for me to ask
for what I need –
just as it is for
everybody else.

BE A NUISANCE

Once you have discovered what you want, don't
be afraid to go out there and get it. Be respectful
of other people's time and listen to a firm 'no', but
don't be afraid to make yourself a bit of a nuisance
to get what you want, whether it's a new job, new
equipment or a place on a training course or team.

First, say to yourself what
you would be, and then
do what you have to do.

Epictetus

PREPARE FOR NEGOTIATIONS

Whether you're looking for a pay rise, an extension on a deadline, or gearing up for an interview, negotiations can feel huge. Do your research beforehand: clarify what you want to achieve and how you can make it happen. Go in with a few different solutions in mind and a fall-back position in case you need it. Make neat, clear notes to take with you and brief yourself on the people you will be negotiating with. Preparation is power.

GET YOUR NEEDS MET

One of the things people can struggle with is feeling that their needs are not valid. What's helpful is to remember the difference between a want and a need: you might *want* a £5,000 pay rise, but you may only *need* £500 more to pay the rent. We *want* the latest smartphone, but we *need* a phone that works.

While it's great to be able to ask for what you want, it can be daunting. Make sure you start by at least sticking firm on what you need. Having your needs met will allow you to live a happier, less stressful life, and you have as much right to that as any other person on the planet. The more you negotiate, the more confident you'll become, and the more likely you are to get what you desire.

KNOW YOUR VALUE

Negotiate from a place of knowing your own objective value. If you find that your self-worth flees under pressure, make a list beforehand of all your skills and qualities. Be assertive, and show the person you are talking to that you know you are worth these changes, and they will believe it too.

I am brave enough
to assert myself.

Be honest

Honesty can be tough. Giving feedback
to someone about something that
they've done wrong or that's making
you uncomfortable is a strong assertion of
your needs – and that's not always easy to
do. Be kind with the truth, and appropriate, but
remain strong: remember your feelings are valid.

TRUST YOURSELF TO SAY NO

When you don't always feel your own value, it can be difficult to trust yourself, but your gut feelings are there for a reason. You know what is right for you and it is good to trust those instincts. Acknowledge when you're afraid of something new and don't let the fear stop you, but also know when a situation has gone too far and is no longer beneficial.

Setting boundaries by saying 'no' is a hugely important skill, but for many reasons people at all levels of confidence can find it hard to do. If you're struggling to say 'no' to someone or something, practise by yourself beforehand, and know you are strong enough to see it through. You don't always have to explain your reasons if the situation doesn't warrant it, just the word 'no' is perfectly valid and should be enough.

With confidence,
you have won before
you have started.

Marcus
Garvey

KICK OUT DOUBT

Don't indulge your self-doubt. Every time you hear a voice telling you what you want and need isn't valid – whether it's from within or from someone else – remind yourself that you have just as much right to feel happy and fulfilled as everybody else. Don't give yourself a hard time if you catch yourself doubting, just give yourself a mental hug and move on to other thoughts.

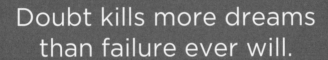

Doubt kills more dreams
than failure ever will.

Suzy
Kassem

Activate your support network

If a situation gets too much, remember you can always ask for help. Turning to friends, family, or colleagues when you need assistance is not an admission of defeat. In fact, asking for help is a sign of strength. What's more, if you make that initial jump in asking for help, you will have the confidence to ask again in future, starting a virtuous cycle. You can even offer support to the people around you, spreading the boosting effects of your own growing self-belief.

I am capable.
I am clever.
I can do this.

GIVING TO OTHER PEOPLE

Giving to others can help you get out of a worrisome headspace. Send flowers to your parents, make a cake for a friend just because, or just help out with housework – whoever you're doing the favour for will feel cared about, and nothing beats the boost of making someone smile! Make sure you don't fall into the trap of over-giving though: it's hard to help anyone if you don't look after yourself first.

When I give to others, the world gives back to me.

CONFIDENT IN THE FUTURE

Your confidence journey doesn't stop at the end of this book. In fact, it's a road you'll keep travelling for your whole life. To help you move forward and keep on heading in a positive direction, here are some tips that look to the future.

Dream lofty dreams,
and as you dream,
so shall you become.

James
Allen

CREATE YOUR FUTURE SELF

Take the time to really figure out what a confident you might look like, what they might be doing and the kind of life they might live. You can just keep this image in your head, as part of a visualisation practice, but it's also a fun, boosting exercise to put it down on paper.

Draw, write about or make a collage of your confident future self. Surround the portrait with things that make you happy, photos of people you love, and images, words and phrases that inspire you. Use it to remind you what you're aiming for. With a good amount of effort, a lot of positivity, and a little bit of luck, you can make that image a reality.

My imagination is the key to my future.

Never give up

Some days are harder than others,
but don't ever give up on becoming
more confident, or living a more peaceful,
happier life. Even in the depths of a bad
phase, know that everything has its own
time, and the good days will come around
again. No matter what setbacks you face, you
can always create another opportunity to live
your dreams. Put faith in the idea that you can
achieve what you want and, eventually, you will!

Trust yourself.
Create the kind of
self that you will be
happy to live
with all your life.

Golda Meir

FORGIVE YOURSELF

Sometimes the person it can be hardest to forgive is yourself. When we don't live up to our own expectations, or feel we have failed someone else, we can really haul ourselves over the coals about it.

Instead, breathe, and focus on being kind to yourself. Ask yourself whether you would give anyone else the same hard time, and if you wouldn't, ask why you're being so harsh on yourself. Your own inner critic is normally the harshest voice you'll ever have to listen to, but you can train it to be more positive with time, patience and courage.

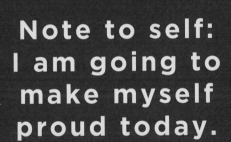

Note to self: I am going to make myself proud today.

KEEP BEING PROUD
OF YOURSELF

Every time you achieve something, remember
to congratulate yourself. Celebrate life and what
you can bring to it, and keep adding to the lists
of things that make you proud. Be your own
biggest fan, because if you don't tell the world
what you can do, it might never find out!

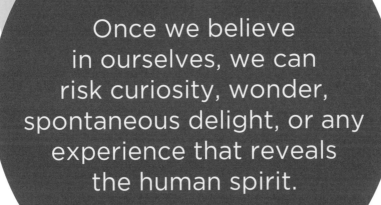

Once we believe
in ourselves, we can
risk curiosity, wonder,
spontaneous delight, or any
experience that reveals
the human spirit.

E. E.
Cummings

REACH OUT FROM A PLACE OF KINDNESS

Whether you're in the depths of nervous insecurity, or the heights of giddy confidence, try to allow yourself to come from a place of kindness. Whatever the situation, whether you're having a hard time standing up for yourself, or you're trying to keep a big work project moving forwards, solutions are always easier to reach when we're kind to one another.

What's more, by helping and being generous towards other people, you're creating a strong network of people who believe in you and whom you believe in. Mutual support creates group confidence, which allows each individual within the group to better reach their goals and dreams, whether it's family, friends or colleagues.

Happiness is a journey,
not a destination.

Anonymous

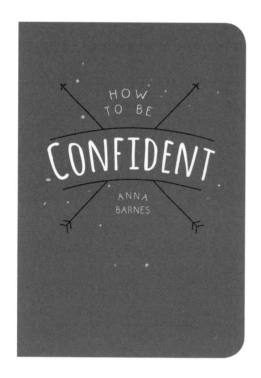

HOW TO BE CONFIDENT
Anna Barnes

£8.99

978-1-84953-795-7

Paperback

Confidence is within your reach

Confidence doesn't come naturally to everyone, and needs to be developed over time. If you struggle to feel calm and poised under pressure, or wish you had the self-assurance to shout about all your star qualities, then look no further: this book is here to help.

Bursting with tips, assertive statements and activities, How to Be Confident will enable you to work through whatever is holding you back so you can embrace your inner confidence.

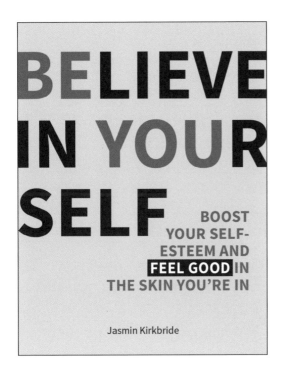

BELIEVE IN YOURSELF
Jasmin Kirkbride

£8.99

978-1-84953-949-4

Hardback

Do you ever wish you had more confidence in your abilities?

Do you sometimes have negative thoughts, comparing yourself to others?

Have you ever been afraid to speak up because you don't think your opinion is valid?

You are not alone, and there is a way to tackle your low self-esteem. Packed with tips, suggestions and quotes, this book will help give you the strength to turn negatives into positives and become more confident every day.

Have you enjoyed this book?
If so, why not write a review on your favourite website?

If you're interested in finding out more about our
books, find us on Facebook at **Summersdale Publishers**
and follow us on Twitter at **@Summersdale**.

Thanks very much for buying this Summersdale book.

www.summersdale.com